The Anatomy Of Feeling

Mapping the Heart

Katie Scott

BookLeaf Publishing

India | USA | UK

Made with ❤ on the BookLeaf Publishing Platform

www.bookleafpub.in

www.bookleafpub.com

Dedication

For the broken, the blooming, and those in between.

Preface

These poems were not written all at once.
They arrived slowly- in the quiet after
heartbreak, in the midst of the chaos of becoming,
in moments I thought I was splintered beyond repair.
This collection is a map of feeling,
 and anatomy of what it means to carry joy and grief in
the same breath.
 Each poem is a fragment, a truth,
a question I may never answer.
 I did not write these to be understood by everyone-
 only to be felt by someone.
 If only one line finds you where you are,
if it rests in the back of your mind
or gives you language for something you couldn't name
before,
then this book has filled its purpose.

Thank you for opening it.
Thank you for opening yourself.

Acknowledgements

To every heartbreak, every moment of stillness, every small joy that became every verse- thank you for showing up.

Rituals of Balance

In the calmness of the morning,
I rise, breathing slow,
a moment carved from chaos,
a space to plant intention deep.

I sip the stillness,
cup in hand,
as the earth absorbs my feet,
its steady pulse reminding me
to root, to center,
to find that delightful place
where the world can bend
but never break.

With each motion, deliberate,
I gather the pieces:
a breath, a thought,
a word spoken with aim.
Balance is a prelude,
a rhythm slow and steady,
between the chaos and calm,
between the wants and needs.

I find the meaning like devotions,

into the dough of the day,
kneading with purpose,
each step, each word,
a choice made with meaning,
not for speed,
but for grace.

In the ritual of living,
there is balance in the waiting,
in the letting go and holding on,
in the knowing
that every moment
is a chance to choose
what stays and what slips away.

The Harvest

The earth stirs softly,
beneath the golden sky,
as the fields run wild,
arms open and ready.

Hands weathered and worn,
gather the fruits of patience,
each grain, each crop,
a testament to the long hours.

Tomato vines rise like pillars,
apples, ripened with sweet nectar,
and the wheat stands tall
keeping the secrets of the soil.

The air is thick with the smell
of earth and rain and time,
as baskets fill,
and the land exhales, peaceful.

It is a harvest of more than crops,
but of memories,
of work worn in strength and heart,
of seasons that gave and took,

and grew again.

We gather not only what grows,
but what has been planted deep-
dreams that took root,
under the sun's eternal watch,
now ripened in the tranquility,
ready to be carried home.

Golden Hour

The sun sinks low,
like a tired traveler slipping
into the quiet comfort of the night,
prisms, like hands combing the horizon
with the tenderest touch.

The sky, once bold,
now softens,
a tapestry of tangerine and rose,
woven with the fading light,
a slow surrender to the night.

The trees stand still,
their branches whistling
in the last breath of warmth,
and the earth below,
a patient companion,
welcomes the night's brush of evening.

I watch, not with longing,
but with gratitude,
for the way the day knows how to let go,
how the sun knows how to rest,
and how we too,

can follow its lead,
trusting the quiet fall
into the peaceful night.

These Mobile Roots

I stood by the lake,
watching the water pluck away the leaves,
each one caught in the current,
no longer grasping,
no longer afraid to let go.

There are people, you see,
who are like stones at the bottom of the stream,
heavy with pride,
held down by their own strife,
and no matter how hard the current pulls,
they refused to be carried.

I have tried-
I have tried to encourage them,
to soften the coarse edges,
to inspire that change is possible,
but some things are meant to stay
where they are,
rooted in their ways.

And so,
I have learned
to let myself float away,

to let the current carry me
to other shores far away.

The lake will flow,
with or without them,
and I will stand here,
free,
knowing that peace comes
when we stop trying to grip
what was never meant to keep us.

The Power of Words

Words are like pebbles-
small enough to slip through your fingers,
but heavy enough to leave a mark.
They tumble from my tongue
rippling across minds you may never meet.

A quiet truth can erode the silence,
a sentence can mend what once was broken,
words wrap around wounds like gauze,
binding the lesions that doubt tried to scorn.

You can raise someone with a phrase,
turn smoke to fresh, crisp air-
show them they are more than the burdens
they carry.
A simple, *I believe you*
can pull someone from the edge.

But words are wild too-
sharp when twisted,
cold when wielded without care.
They can cut deeper than silence,
leaving scars unseen.

So speak as if your words leave imprint-
soft enough to mediate,
strong enough to last.
Because language is not just sound-
it is the gateways you build
between hearts that crave mending.

When You Speak In Flames

Your words strike the air
like flint against stone—
sharp, cutting, seething
into something too hot
to hold.

I watch the fire build,
watch this stake turn black
with the clap of your anger.
You say it is nothing,
but I can feel the heat
climbing up my skin.

Once your voice
was a place I ran to
for comfort and guidance.
Now, it is a thunder
I brace for,

waiting for the blaze
to pass my by,
to spare my fervent mind
and tinsel heart.

My words evaporate
as you spin and clash
around the room.
The more you say, the more clearly I see-
this is your goodbye to me.

The One Who Watched

You were there-
not in the way of a storm,
not in the way of a hand raised in anger,
but in the way of silence,
a door left open,
the blinds never drawn.

You sat in the benevolent light of the morning,
while shadows moved in the next room,
while voices sharpened to pitchforks,
while I shrank smaller and smaller,
waiting for a word, a gesture,
some small act to pacify.

But you only rifled through papers,
poured your coffee,
and spoke of the weather,
as if the walls were not shaking,
as if your silence
was not another form of violence.

And now, years later,
I think of you not with anger,
but with something colder-

the thought
that those who cover their eyes
are just as dangerous
as those who do the harm.

Golden Armor

I once thought protection meant hardness-
a shield thick as iron,
a citadel entrenched against the earth.
But the trees have taught me otherwise,
how they bend with nature's warm breeze
and still they do not break.

So I have hammered my armor from gold,
fashioned it neatly over my body-
heavy and rigid,
but light as the morning sun
spilling across the open fields.
It is made of every kindness I have given,
every wound I healed instead of hardened,
every time I chose to ascend despite my faults.

Let the world come with its storms,
its sharp tongues and careless minds-
I do not fear the battles.
I glean. I shimmer. I shine.
Walking forward,
wrapped in all the light
I have ever given away.

Turning Away

I've learned to turn my back on you,
not because I wanted to,
but because your actions unlocked battle cries
that echoed across lifetimes unseen.

Each Lifetime, a chapter,
each turn, a lesson in survival.
In knowing when words morph into something
that no longer nourish,
but instead foster maladies,
and fill corners with doubt
where once there was trust.

In this lifetime, the weight of your choices
pulled us further from the scales of
balance,
turning the key, locking the door
I never wanted to close.

But now, it's clear:
this turning is not an escape,
but a lifetime of change-
a step toward who I must become,
without the knowledge of your journey.

Each time I walk away,
a little piece of me heals,
a little piece of you fades away,
until in the next life,
where there's no need to turn-
because I'll have learned
how to walk on without you,
with no fear or worry,
only the lessons of each lifetime
carved into every path I take.

Learning to Roar

I used to say
my guiding animal was an otter-
full of joy and nimble humor,
twisting through currents,
finding laughter in the gentle flow.
I wanted to be that simple,
to drift with the tide,
to trust the water to steer me home.

But somewhere along the way
the rivers ran shallow,
the rocks cut deeper,
and the shoreline felt too far.
I learned that playfulness
does not always keep you safe-
sometimes you need claws.

But the grizzly bear guides me now.
She does not ask permission to take up space.
Her footsteps reverberate through the earth,
her breath clouds the air.
She moves with slow and determined power,
her strength not something she flaunts-
but something you *know.*

I have learned to stand my ground,
to speak with my whole chest
when something threatens what I love.
I am no longer all softness and tender joy-
I am teeth and spine,
I am wild and unworried,
I am the kind of force that stands tall and does not back
down.

Artist's Palette

Out here, the desert dreams in color-
not soft pastels,
but bold confessions
splashed across stone
like a painter lost in feeling.

Artist's Palette-
where the earth lets go,
spills its secrets
in swirls of rose, jade, and gold,
and that sweet lavender
that only shows up
when the sun's at the right angle
and the air is clear.

This is where nature speaks in layers,
where time unfolds
to show its value,
its fire,
its minerals formed to memory.

No brush touched this.
No hand guided it.
Just heat and pressure,

wind and ash,
erosion and eruption-
chaos turned to masterpiece.

You stand there,
small,
bewildered,
thinking this must be what truth looks like
when it isn't trying to be beautiful,
but is anyway.

Colors born of ferocity
sit soft against the cliffs,
and it makes me wonder
what parts of you
could be stunning too,
if anyone saw them in the right light.

The Earthbound Alchemist

Early in the evening,
as a chaotic world stirs,
She kneels on the earth,
palms open, cradling the roots
as if offering her humble prayer.

The sun leans in,
watching the way she presses the earth
gently but firmly-
a quiet form of alchemy.

She does not rush.
She hums,
a tune nature discerns best,
as she tucks each fragile stem
into its place.

Later, the rain will come,
soft fingers tapping the leaves.
The flowers will bloom,
lifting their bright faces to the sky,
always knowing whose hands
first gave them a home.

The Gentle Violinist

He sits in the corner,
bow set firmly between his fingers,
the wood of his violin worn soft
from years of mindful practice.

Outside, the world pours-
wind knocking at the windows,
rain spilling from a sky
that never seems to hold back.

But still, he plays.

The strings resound like a heartbeat
steady, unwavering,
each note rising
from a place he's kept safe
when everything else felt unraveled.

The roof once leaked above his head.
The cold once claimed his bones.
The world once told him to stop-
that no one would listen.

But still, he plays.

Because the music know his name,
knows his heart,
knows he is more than what has tried
to keep him.

And when his bow skims the strings,
the room softens-
the storm quiets-
and his gentle song carries
like a pulse
that refuses to be silenced.

Pedals of the Past

I gather the pieces-
dusted keys, splintered wood,
stories echoed through generations,
each one a beam
laid down with focused hands.

The chambers of voices linger,
like hymns through the pipes-
my sister's laughter,
my father's symphony,
my mother's earnest strength
welded into each piece.

I sift through memories,
choosing what to carry forward:
the wisdom of roots,
the courage of storms,
the resilience that fervors a heartbeat
beneath the shifted foundation.

Not all of it fits-
some iron fades in my hand,
worn too thin by time and strain.
I leave those behind,

knowing that everything
has the chance to rebuild.

Instead, I line new walls,
plastering them with hope,
nailing down love like the
pieces reborn.

This home-
this life-
is a careful nod to the old one.
And when the wind stirs the trees
and their branches tap the glass,
I hear the voices still-
the ones who came before-
and know I have made room for them here
in the purpose of what I've built.

Bella Famiglia

The scent rises first-
garlic kissed by heat,
tomatoes simmering low and slow,
their exuberance thickening the air
like a story shared a hundred times.

The kitchen offers melodies of sweet bliss-
a wooden spoon stirring past to present,
my mother's hands guiding my own
even now, years have gone by but never too far.

The dough is soft yet stubborn,
just like her.
"Patience," she said,
her fingers folding love with every crease,
each strain of pasta, a simple promise
that family is built upon one bite at a time.

Wine pours freely- ruby and rich-
voices fill and fall like waves.
Laughter spills louder than sauce from the pot,
and no one minds.
This is home- wild, radiant, and full of heart.

We eat like we're tasting culture itself-
basil plucked fresh from the garden,
cheese sharp enough to bit back,
bread torn by hand and passed around
like offerings of peace.

Each plate reminds me:
we are more than names in a family line-
we are simmered and seasoned,
layered with love,
engraved with stories
and crafted with warmth.

The Ones Who Stay

Some people arrive like lightning-
bright, electric, unforgettable-
but gone before you find
how to hold the glow.

But then there are the ones
who embrace you like roots-
quiet, steady, weaving themselves
into your foundation.

The friends who've seen you
through every season-
when your branches are bare,
when your leaves flare gold,
when your petals spring forward,
and when you're nothing
but tangled thorns

They are the voices
that know your silence,
the hands that lift
without asking why,
the hearts that stay
when your own feels too heavy to grasp.

There's no need to count the years-
time becomes something smaller with them-
not measured in months
but in shared stories,
ecstatic conversations,
and the comfort of knowing
that when the world feels too thunderous,
they will always be
your quiet place to land.

The Quiet Deliverance

They called you quiet,
but never noticed the steel beneath your
stillness.
For years, their words flung like stones,
each one landing, bruising-
but never breaking.

You walked away, head bowed,
but you kept your wits,
gathering the receipts they tried to deny.
You learned the rhythm of their cruelty,
the way their laughter sharpened on edges,
the way rumors turned your name
into something twisted.

And then, one day-
when they thought you'd wilted for good,

you rose.

Not in rage, but in clarity.
You spoke, steady as a drum,
each word slicing through their smirks.
No shouting, no venom-

just truth, cold and clean.

Their faces worn,
caught in the mirror you held up.
They stumbled over the weight of their own
words,
and you stood taller than ever,
the quiet one who knew when to strike.

Not to hurt,
but to remind them-
you were never broken.

The Art of Letting Go

I have spent too many mornings
with worry curled inside of me,
its prickly breath in my ear,
whispering all the ways
my world could break.

But outside, the river keeps moving.
The heron lifts its majestic wings.
The moon does not ask
what comes next—
it waxes and wanes to its own
divine rhythm.

And oh, to live like that—
to loosen my grip,
to trust the sky, the stars
to find its natural alignment
to hold its own weight,
and carry mine too.

The Phoenix

From the ashes, you rise-
not as you were,
but as you *will* be,
stronger than before,
a shadow of your former glory
scorched away by fire.

Each flame,
a glimmer of what you've lost,
but each ember,
a spark of what is to come-
the phoenix,
reborn in its own fire,
finding wings where once were none.

You are healing in the flames,
rising from the ashes,
with every breath
that pulls you higher,
every tear
that builds you stronger,
and every flight that brings you
 closer to the sky.

Humble Reminders

The wound speaks softly,
not in cries of pain,
but in a tearful whisper-
humble reminders of what was lost,
and what was found.

It teaches you to dance with forgiveness,
not in great absolution,
but in small gentle moments
of letting go.

Healing is the act of listening
to what the wound has weeped,
and then,
with courage,
allowing yourself
to move forward.

The scar will remain,
but it will not define you.
It will simply be
another part of your story-
the part where you healed.

Hands on The Horizon

There was a time when the wind took everything,
the storm swept through to leave me barren,
when my own hands, empty, and shaken,
forgot how to carry,
how to hold on.

I have known the language of destruction,
of falling,
of reading the names of my own scars
like the phantoms who are seen.

But today, the sun finds me standing.
Not untouched, nor unscathed-
but here.
The earth hums beneath my feet,
whispering: *you made it.*

And I have.

Not because I fought harder,
not because I deserved more,
but because somewhere inside of me,
where the burden once lived,
something new began to grow.

Call it grace, call it will,
call it the simple, stubborn truth
that even the most tangled beings
can still strive for hope and love and joy
with every lifetime.